JERMYN STREET THEATRE

Mary's Babies

by Maud Dromgoole

Jermyn Street Theatre
20 March – 13 April, 2019
Press performance Friday 22 March

Mary's Babies
by Maud Dromgoole

CAST

CAROLINE, ETHEL, RITA, JAMES, SUZIE, REGISTRAR, HENRY, GRETA, HANNAH, CHARLOTTE, MILLY, LIBERTY, GERTIE, RACHEL, CELIA, SUSAN, LUKE, MARCUS   Emma Fielding

KIERAN, BRET, GRACIE, SOPHIE, REBECCA, VENTRILOQUIST, TOM, SARAH, LINDA, MICHAEL, JOSEPH, HARRY, VERITY, JACK, JOHN, LIZZIE, KATE, PAUL, SAM, PETER, ERIC, EMMA, KEITH   Katy Stephens

PRODUCTION TEAM

Director	Tatty Hennessy
Designer	Anna Reid
Lighting Designer	Jai Morjaria
Sound Designer	Yvonne Gilbert
Casting Director	Matilda James
Assistant Director	Kennedy Bloomer
Production Manager	Cameron Murray for eStage
Stage Manager	Caroline Lowe
Production Photographer	Robert Workman

Produced and general managed by Jermyn Street Theatre in a co-production with Oak Theatre.

With thanks to the Donor Conception Network, Pride Angel and support from the Thomas Arno Foundation and Arts Council England.

Supported by
ARTS COUNCIL ENGLAND

Previous productions of *Mary's Babies* were produced by Hannah Tookey and have included:

The Vaults, January 2018
CAROLINE, ETHEL, RITA, etc   Rhiannon Neads
KIERAN, BRET, GRACIE, etc   Deli Segal

Fertility Fest, Bush Theatre, May 2018
KIERAN, BRET, GRACIE, etc   Sian Martin
CAROLINE, ETHEL, RITA, etc   Karina Fernandez

King's Head, July 2018
KIERAN, BRET, GRACIE, etc   Caoilfhionn Dunne
CAROLINE, ETHEL, RITA, etc   Ellie Piercy

Cast

EMMA FIELDING | CAROLINE, ETHEL, RITA, JAMES, SUZIE, REGISTRAR, HENRY, GRETA, HANNAH, CHARLOTTE, MILLY, LIBERTY, GERTIE, RACHEL, CELIA, SUSAN, LUKE, MARCUS

Theatre includes: *A Woman of No Importance* (West End); *Terror* (Lyric Hammersmith); *The Massive Tragedy of Madame Bovary* (Liverpool Everyman/Peepolykus); *Rapture Blister Burn* (Hampstead Theatre); *In the Republic of Happiness*, *Spinning Into Butter* (Royal Court Theatre); *The King's Speech* (Wyndham's Theatre); *Heartbreak House* (Chichester Festival Theatre); *Playing With Fire, Look Back In Anger, Arcadia* (National Theatre); *Rock 'N' Roll* (Duke of York's Theatre); *Private Lives* (Albery Theatre/ Broadway – Theater World Award, Olivier Award Nomination); *Decade* (Headlong); *Macbeth, Heartbreak House, 1953, School for Wives* (Almeida Theatre); *Revolt She Said, Revolt Again, Cymbeline, Measure for Measure, The School for Scandal* (Olivier Award nomination), *Twelfth Night, A Midsummer Night's Dream, The Broken Heart* (Royal Shakespeare Company).

Television includes: *Years & Years, Les Miserables, Unforgotten, Silent Witness, Dark Angel, Close to the Enemy, Capital, Arthur & George, This Is England '90, Foyle's War, DCI Banks, Silk, The Game, George Gently, Death in Paradise, The Suspicions of Mr Whicher, Kidnap & Ransom, Cranford, Fallen Angel, Beneath the Skin, The Government Inspector, Waking the Dead, My Uncle Silas, Other People's Children, A Respectable Trade, A Dance to the Music of Time, Drover's Gold, Poirot.*

Film includes: *Fast Girls, The Other Man, Discovery of Heaven, Pandaemonium.*

Emma is an associate artist with the Royal Shakespeare Company.

KATY STEPHENS | KIERAN, BRET, GRACIE, SOPHIE, REBECCA, VENTRILOQUIST, TOM, SARAH, LINDA, MICHAEL, JOSEPH, HARRY, VERITY, JACK, JOHN, LIZZIE, KATE, PAUL, SAM, PETER, ERIC, EMMA, KEITH

Theatre includes: *Antony and Cleopatra* (National Theatre); *A View from the Bridge, Macbeth* (Tobacco Factory Theatres); *IHO* (Hampstead Theatre); *The Histories Cycle, As You Like It, Antony and Cleopatra, King Lear, Titus Andronicus, The Taming of the Shrew, Candide, The Grain Store, Forests* (Royal Shakespeare Company); *The Oresteia, Julius Caesar, Dr. Scroggy's War, Thomas Tallis, The Complete Walk* (*Antony and Cleopatra*) (Shakespeare's Globe); *Othello* (Shakespeare at the Tobacco Factory); *Hamlet* (Trafalgar Studios); *The King's Speech* (Chichester Festival Theatre/ Birmingham Rep); *Tamburlaine* (Bristol Old Vic/Barbican); and various seasons at the Colchester Mercury Theatre and Belgrade Theatre, Coventry.

Television and film includes: *The Bill, Ellington* (ITV); *London's Burning* (LWT); *Fun Song Factory* (CITV); *Prick Thy Neighbour, Relative Values* (Overseas Film Group).

Katy is an associate artist with the Royal Shakespeare Company and with Kelly Hunter's Flute Theatre. She also runs BOLD AS BARD, a Shakespeare theatre Company for adults with learning disabilities.

Production Team

MAUD DROMGOOLE | WRITER

Theatre includes: *3 Billion Seconds* (VAULT Festival); *Rosa, Ursula and Richard* (Finalist Mercury Weinberger Prize, reading at Old Red Lion Theatre); *Blue Moon* (Bread and Roses/The Courtyard Theatre/Arcola Theatre).

Short plays include: *Sleeping Beauty* (The Bunker); *Milk* (The Bunker/Hackney Attic); *Cake* (The Cockpit/Tristan Bates Theatre); *The Boy James* (Love Bites); *A Violet in the Youth of Primy Nature* (Theatre 20th Utopia); *Selkie* (Southwark Playhouse/Old Red Lion Theatre).

Her sitcom *Acting Up* was shortlisted for BBC Writersroom Comedy Script Room and her short films include *Portrait of a Bride; Second Skin; Nightingale and the Queen*.

TATTY HENNESSY | DIRECTOR

Theatre includes: *The Road Behind, The Road Ahead* (The Theatre, Chipping Norton); *As You Like It, Romeo and Juliet* (Shakespeare in the Squares); *The Snow Queen* (Theatre N16); *Acorn* (The Courtyard Theatre).

Assistant direction includes: *Fanny and Alexander* (Old Vic); *Hamlet* (Shakespeare's Globe/world tour); *An Audience with Jimmy Savile* (Park Theatre); *Cinderella* (Lyric Theatre); *The Duchess of Malfi* (Sam Wanamaker Playhouse).

Tatty's own play, *A Hundred Words for Snow*, is currently playing at the Trafalgar Studios.

ANNA REID | DESIGNER

For Jermyn Street Theatre: *Dry Land*.

Other theatre includes: *Our Country's Good, A Midsummer Night's Dream* (Tobacco Factory Theatre, Bristol); *Paradise, The Hoes* (Hampstead Theatre); *Twelfth Night, The Sweet Science of Bruising, Collective Rage, Dear Brutus, The Cardinal, School Play* (Southwark Playhouse); *Dust, Rasheeda Speaking* (Trafalgar Studios); *Soft Animals, Drip Feed, Fury, Brute* (Soho Theatre); *Schism* (Park Theatre); *Grotty* (The Bunker); *Tiny Dynamite* (Old Red Lion Theatre); *Rattle Snake* (Live Theatre Newcastle/York Theatre Royal/Soho Theatre); *The Kitchen Sink, Jumpers for Goalposts* (The Oldham Coliseum); *Sex Worker's Opera* (set only, national tour/Ovalhouse); *I'm Gonna Pray For You So Hard* (Finborough Theatre); *Arthur's World* (Bush Theatre); *Hippolytos* (Victoria and Albert Museum); *Hamlet* (The Riverside Studios).

JAI MORJARIA | LIGHTING DESIGNER

Lighting designs include: *Glory* (Duke's Theatre, Lancaster/Red Ladder); *Cuzco, Scrooge and the Seven Dwarves* (Theatre503); *The Hoes* (Hampstead Theatre); *Losing Venice* (Orange Tree Theatre); *King Lear, Lorna Doone* (Exmoor National Park); *Sufi:Zen* (Akademi Dance); *No Sound Ever Dies* (Surrey Arts); *Superhero: The Musical* (NYMT); *Engine Break* (The Plasticine Men); *Kanye The First* (HighTide); *Robin Hood* (Greenwich Theatre); *Alice in Wonderland* (Birmingham Old Rep); *Bitched* (Kali); *A Lie of the Mind, A Midsummer Night's Dream* (Southwark Playhouse); *The Cunning Little Vixen* (Arcola Theatre/The Opera Company); *My Name is Rachel Corrie* (The Other Room, Cardiff); *46 Beacon* (Trafalgar Studios with Rick Fisher); *Out There on Fried Meat Ridge Road* (White Bear Theatre/Trafalgar Studios 2); *Acorn* (Courtyard Theatre; OffWestEnd Award nomination – Best Lighting); *The Man Will Kill Us All, The Crucible* (ALRA); *The Legend of Charlie Peace* (Central); *The Beggar's Opera, Pains of Youth, Obama-ology* (RADA).

Jai trained at RADA and won the 2016 Association of Lighting Designer's ETC Award.

YVONNE GILBERT | SOUND DESIGNER

For Jermyn Street Theatre: *Parents' Evening, Hymn to Love* (also Theatre by the Lake), *The Last Ones*.

Theatre includes: *Coming Clean* (Trafalgar Studios); *Hansel and Gretel* (The Rose Theatre, Kingston); *Giselle* (English National Ballet); *ShirleyManda* (Playground Theatre); *Moonfleet* (Salisbury Playhouse); *Oranges and Elephants* (Hoxton Hall); *I Loved Lucy* (Arts Theatre); *Coming Clean* (King's Head Theatre); *Urinetown* (The Pleasance); *Guess How Much I Love You* (Greenwich Theatre); *Murder, Margaret and Me* (York Theatre Royal); *Romeo and Juliet, Much Ado about Nothing* (Rose Playhouse); *The Nativity* (St James Church); *Romeo and Juliet* (Clywd, New Theatre); *Brideshead Revisited* (York Theatre Royal); *Jacques Brel* (Mountview); *Ghost* (Ivy Arts Centre); *Man of La Mancha, Legally Blonde, American Idiot* (Bridewell Theatre); *Singer/Touched* (Bernie Grants Arts Centre); *Eighth Wonder of the World* (Brunel Museum); *Carousel* (Royal Academy of Music); *On the Town, Addams Family Musical, Lift, Rent* (Ivy Arts Centre); *Twelfth Night* (Regent's Park Open Air Theatre); *King James Bible, Statement of Regret* (National Theatre); *Breed* (Theatre503).

As an Associate: *Macbeth* (Shakespeare's Globe); *Long Day's Journey into Night* (Bristol Old Vic); *Peter and Alice, Privates on Parade* (Noël Coward Theatre); *A Chorus Line* (London Palladium); *Finding Neverland* (Leicester Curve); *Juno and the Paycock* (National Theatre).

MATILDA JAMES | CASTING DIRECTOR

Matilda is currently Associate Producer at Shakespeare's Globe. She was Casting Director there for over four years, casting more than 50 shows for the Globe and Sam Wanamaker Playhouse.

Recent theatre includes: *A Woman of No Importance*, *Lady Windermere's Fan* (Classic Spring at the Vaudeville Theatre); *Farinelli and the King* (Sam Wanamaker Playhouse/West End); *Nell Gwynn* (Shakespeare's Globe/West End); *Hamlet Globe to Globe* (Shakespeare's Globe, touring to every country in the world).

Film casting includes *Benjamin*, *Pond Life*, *Undercliffe* (Open Palm Films) and *The Complete Walk* (37 short films made for the Shakespeare 400 celebrations).

KENNEDY BLOOMER | ASSISTANT DIRECTOR

For Jermyn Street Theatre: *Original Death Rabbit* – Assistant Director.

Directing credits include: *When It Happens* (Tristan Bates Theatre); *Healing Wounds* (Wardown Park House); *Mouth Wide Shut* (Moors Bar); *The Roundheads* (Moseley Old Hall); *Oh No It Isn't* (The Hope Theatre); *Broken* (Old Red Lion Theatre); *TüManz TüK18* (Leicester Square Theatre) *Pareidolia* (Karamel Club).

Assistant directing credits include: *There but for the grace of God – (go I)* (Soho Theatre/Camden People's Theatre/ARC, Stockton); *Foul Pages* (The Hope Theatre); *Thark* (Drayton Arms Theatre); *Comedy of Errors* (Karamel Club).

Producing credits include: *Th'Importance of Bein' Earnest* (Drayton Arms).

JERMYN
STREET
THEATRE

Jermyn Street Theatre is celebrating its twenty-fifth birthday in 2019.

During the 1930s, the basement of 16b Jermyn Street – close to Piccadilly in the heart of London's West End – was home to the glamorous Monseigneur Restaurant and Club. The space was converted into a theatre by Howard Jameson and Penny Horner in the early 1990s, and Jermyn Street Theatre staged its first production in August 1994. The theatre director Neil Marcus became the first Artistic Director in 1995 and secured Lottery funding for the venue; the producer Chris Grady also made a major contribution to the theatre's development. In the late 1990s, the Artistic Director was David Babani, later the founder and Artistic Director of the Menier Chocolate Factory.

Over the last twenty-five years, the theatre has established itself as one of London's leading Off-West End studio theatres, with hit productions including *Barefoot in the Park* with Alan Cox and Rachel Pickup, directed by Sally Hughes, and *Helping Harry* with Adrian Lukis and Simon Dutton, directed by Nickolas Grace. Gene David Kirk, accompanied by Associate Director Anthony Biggs, became Artistic Director in the late 2000s and reshaped the theatre's creative output with revivals of rarely performed plays, including Charles Morgan's post-war classic *The River Line*, the UK premiere of Ibsen's first performed play *St John's Night*, and another Ibsen, *Little Eyolf* starring Imogen Stubbs and Doreen Mantle. Tom Littler staged two acclaimed Stephen Sondheim revivals: *Anyone Can Whistle*, starring Issy van Randwyck and Rosalie Craig, and *Saturday Night*, which transferred to the Arts Theatre.

In 2012, Trevor Nunn directed the world premiere of Samuel Beckett's radio play *All That Fall*, starring Eileen Atkins and Michael Gambon. The production subsequently transferred to the Arts Theatre and then to New York's 59E59 Theatre. Jermyn Street Theatre was nominated for the Peter Brook Empty Space Award in 2011 and won The Stage 100 Best Fringe Theatre in 2012. Anthony Biggs became Artistic Director in 2013, combining his love of rediscoveries with a new focus on emerging artists and writers from outside the UK. Revivals included Eugene O'Neill's early American work *The First Man*, Terence Rattigan's first play *First Episode*, John Van Druten's First World War drama *Flowers of the Forest*, and a repertory season of South African drama. New works include US playwright Ruby Rae Spiegel's *Dry Land*, Jonathan Lewis's *A Level Playing Field*, and Sarah Daniels' *Soldiers' Wives* starring Cath Shipton.

In 2017, Jermyn Street Theatre started a bold new chapter, becoming the West End's newest and smallest producing theatre. Under the leadership of Artistic Director and Executive Producer Tom Littler, a small in-house producing team create or co-produce all the theatre's productions. Partnerships have been forged with numerous regional theatres including English Theatre Frankfurt, Guildford Shakespeare Company, the Stephen Joseph Theatre, Theatre by the Lake, Theatre Royal Bath, the Watermill Theatre, and York Theatre Royal.

Jermyn Street Theatre's first two years as a producing theatre have seen five seasons of work: the Escape, Scandal, Reaction, Rebels, and Portrait Seasons. These have included fifteen world premieres, European premieres of American drama, several major rediscoveries, Christmas comedies, and acclaimed new translations of classic plays. The theatre is committed to equal gender representation both onstage and offstage. It is also committed to paying a fair and legal wage, and has a bespoke agreement with the industry union, Equity. A Director's Circle of private donors is key to the theatre's survival and growth.

In 2018, Littler directed the most ambitious project in the theatre's history – the first complete London revival since 1936 of Noël Coward's nine-play cycle *Tonight at 8.30*. Deputy Director Stella Powell-Jones brought *Tomorrow at Noon* to the stage – three contemporary responses to Coward's work by female playwrights. The two productions ran side-by-side leading to thirty-six one-act plays performed each week, with tremendously popular trilogy days on Saturdays and Sundays.

Throughout its history, the theatre's founders, Howard Jameson and Penny Horner, have continued to serve as Chair of the Board and Executive Director respectively, and the generous donors, front-of-house staff, and tireless volunteers all play their parts in the Jermyn Street Theatre story.

SUPPORT JERMYN STREET THEATRE

Everybody needs their best friends, and every theatre needs them too. At Jermyn Street Theatre we have recently started a Director's Circle. Limited to twenty-five individuals or couples, these are the people we rely on most. They sponsor productions, fund new initiatives, and support our staff. It is a pleasure to get to know them: we invite Director's Circle members to our exclusive press nights and parties, and we often have informal drinks or suppers in small groups. They are also an invaluable sounding board for me. Currently, members of the Director's Circle donate between £2,000 and £55,000 (with a threshold of £2,000 to join). They are our heroes and they make everything possible. We have space at the table for more, and I would love to hear from you.

Tom Littler
Artistic Director

tomlittler@jermynstreettheatre.co.uk

THE DIRECTOR'S CIRCLE

Anonymous
Michael & Gianni Alen-Buckley
Philip & Christine Carne
Jocelyn Abbey & Tom Carney
Colin Clark
Flora Fraser
Charles Glanville & James Hogan
Marjorie Simonds-Gooding
Peter Soros & Electra Toub
Martin Ward & Frances Card
Robert Westlake & Marit Mohn
Melanie Vere Nicoll

AT JERMYN STREET THEATRE

Find us at www.jermynstreettheatre.co.uk @JSTheatre
Box Office: 020 7287 2875
16b Jermyn Street, London SW1Y 6ST

MARY'S BABIES

Maud Dromgoole

Acknowledgements

It's not been an easy birth and I couldn't have done it without:

The stories and advice of

Lucy Blake, the Centre for Family Research Cambridge,
Nina Barnsley and everyone at the Donor Conception Network,
Jessica & Gabby, Kazuko, Nicky and everyone at Fertility Fest,
Erica from Pride Angel and most importantly the three hundred
anonymous, honest, terrifying, generous contributors to my
survey.

The wonderful actors who've helped mould these characters

Lucy Pickles, Deli Segal, Rhiannon Neads, Karina Fernandez,
Sian Martin, Ellie Piercy, Caoilfhionn Dunne, Katy Stephens
and Emma Fielding.

The extraordinary dramaturgy of

My wonderful friend Map Perry, Jessica Dromgoole, Gill Greer,
Linda McLean, Alice Birch, Sarah Daniels, Jenny Bakst,
Nathan Ellis, Joel MacCormack, and everyone at Playgroup.

Also

Matilda James, Josh McTaggart, Jai Morjaria, Hugh Bonneville,
Tom Stoppard, Jack Bradley, Sebastian Baczkiewicz, Rebecca
Gwyther and Celia De Wolff.

Thank you to

Matt, Sarah Liisa, Jodi, Tamara and everyone else at Nick Hern.

Everyone at Jermyn Street, especially Tom Littler, Stella
Powell-Jones, Kennedy Bloomer and most of all Penny Horner
who makes me feel just as welcome as a writer as she has
countless times as a stage manager.

The ever thoughtful Peter and Vivien Mott.

Lastly, my partner in crime, my altruistic egg, Tatty Hennessy.

M.D.

For Jessica, Cat, Billy, Jen, Jenny, Matilda, Maeve & Gordon,
Flora, Sean, Janie, Agnes, Somerset, Dom, Sasha, Siofra,
Grainne, Cara, Pat & June, Sue & Mogs, Chris, Ed, Oli, June
& John, Andy, Julie, Paula and the boys, Chris, Camilla, Felix,
the Cronks, the Dromgooles, and sundry others who make up
my hotchpotch family, genetic and not.

Characters

KIERAN
BRET
CAROLINE
GRACIE
ETHEL
RITA
SOPHIE
JAMES
REBECCA
SUZIE
MARCUS
KEITH
VENTRILOQUIST
REGISTRAR
SARAH
GRETA
LINDA
MICHAEL
JOSEPH
HANNAH
HARRY
VERITY
CHARLOTTE
JOHN
LUKE
LIZZIE
MILLY
KATE
LIBERTY
PAUL
SAM
RACHEL
CELIA

SUSAN
ERIC
EMMA
TOM
HENRY
GERTIE

Author's Note

This play is inspired by the story of Mary Barton and her
husband, Bertold Wiesner. It has been researched through
survey, interview, and consultation with the Donor Conception
Network. Some stories have been recycled with explicit
permission, but the play is an exercise of imagination; a work of
complete fiction and no characters are based on any real people.

There are many characters played by two actors.

Characters' names are represented on stage and illuminated to
the audience to show who is on stage:

Track 1: Kieran, Bret, Gracie, Sophie, Rebecca, Ventriloquist,
Tom, Sarah, Linda, Michael, Joseph, Harry, Verity, Jack, John,
Lizzie, Kate, Paul, Sam, Peter, Eric, Emma, Keith

Track 2: Caroline, Ethel, Rita, James, Suzie, Registrar, Henry,
Greta, Hannah, Charlotte, Milly, Liberty, Gertie, Rachel, Celia,
Susan, Luke, Marcus

All characters should be conceivable conceived at the Barton
clinic operational from the late '30s until 1967, making them at
the time of the play's setting (2007) between the ages of forty
and eighty.

Words in [square brackets] are unspoken.

A forward slash (/) indicates an interruption, including
a self-interruption.

*This text went to press before the end of rehearsals and so may
differ slightly from the play as performed.*

1. KIERAN

It's 2007.

Oranges are orange.

Humans share fifty per cent of their DNA with a banana.

Which are yellow.

There are twenty-four hours in a day.

A limerick has five lines.

My name is Kieran Taylor.

I don't like Tomatoes.

The five-year survival rate of stage-two breast cancer is sixty-two per cent.

Thirty-eight per cent is not negligible.

Humans share ninety-nine per cent of DNA with each other, only one per cent makes us unique.

Karen Taylor was born in London 1935.

We share ninety-nine-point-five per cent of our DNA with our parents.

Karen was evacuated to Wales in 1940 and her parents perished in the Blitz in 1943. Karen stayed in Wales and became a maid.

She liked Bakewell tart.

She disliked figs.

She died on Monday at 13:52.

Those things I think are true.

A life is made of facts and for the most part they carry equal weight. You care as much that an apricot has a stone as you do that three thousand children a day die from malaria. They are facts. You don't particularly engage with them. If your daughter were one of the three thousand you'd probably care immensely about the malaria, and if you were choking on your fruit salad you'd probably care immensely about the stone. But for the most part they are both just facts.

But if you found out that malaria had never existed.

Or that apricots had never had stones.

Everyone had just told you that they did.

Then you'd be cross.
You might start to wonder about peaches too. And smallpox.

I find being lied to about facts very disorientating. If someone
tells you they have a boyfriend when they don't then that can be
disheartening. If someone tells you they're your mother all your
life and then it turns out that they're not, well that can be,
disheartening. This may not be the time to do this, but No
legacy is as rich as honesty so.

When the facts that you think you know turn out to be lies it's
like a little earthquake, a little earthquake that brings big
buildings crashing down.

These buildings need to be rebuilt from the foundations. Proper
facts. Solid enough to build a house on. Solid enough to build
a Life on.

The cornerstone is the first stone set in the construction of
any masonry foundation. It is very important. It is important
because all other stones will be set in reference to this stone.
The cornerstone determines the entire structure.
Most of your cornerstones will involve sex between your
mother and your father. Probably in a bed.
Maybe somewhere else.
My cornerstone involves no sex at all.
My cornerstone is laid in a Medical Clinic in London run by
a woman named Mary Barton and her husband Bertold Wiesner.
The pair were pioneers of artificial insemination and helped one
thousand five hundred women to conceive.
In 1962 a woman named Beatrice Miller persuaded her husband
Samuel to visit Mary and Bertold and in 1963 I was born.
Samuel in recognition that I wasn't his would not have me in
the house and I was taken by their maid.
Who you know, who was Karen.
Karen then deceived me in regard to my heritage for the next
forty-four years until about six months ago. Unfortunately by
then my mother Beatrice was already dead, but at least I had
a half a cornerstone.
In the early days, donor conception was a very secretive affair.
Finding my father has been very challenging. No parents were
allowed to know who their donor was and they advised them
never to tell their children. Mary and Bertold destroyed all of

their records. But the scarcity of donors meant they relied on a very small pool of men. I thought I might have been their friend Derek Richter's son, who has an estimated one hundred children. But, eh. A recent DNA test has proved that I am in fact the son of Bertold himself. As well as likely some one thousand others. I have. One thousand brothers and sisters. Out there. Somewhere. Maybe even one of you.

I did love Karen.

And I did not know she would die.

But I think it is inappropriate for me to be giving this Eulogy. As I was not her son. I won't be at the wake. If you will excuse me I have some family to find. They could be anywhere. They could be anyone.

CAROLINE *enters. They lock eyes and* KIERAN *grows a bit taller.* KIERAN *assumes a more muscular, more confident stance. He takes his clothes off to become* BRET. *They kiss.* BRET *cups* CAROLINE's *head and pushes her down on to a bed.*

2. BRET & CAROLINE

He is lying on top of her. We can't see her face as his elbows are either side.

BRET *moves mechanically.*

He grunts hesitantly.

About once every five seconds.

A bit like he's trying to work out a poo.

CAROLINE   Oop sorry. I just. No it's fine I just. Could I go on top, I'm feeling a little bit.

BRET   Oh um... That better?

CAROLINE   Yeah, yeah, just wanted to... stifled.

She is on top of him. He is uncertain; less comfortable in this position. He pulls his hands into her hips and starts to move her around a little. She clumsily attempts her own rhythms but gives up.

BRET   Who's your daddy.

He spanks her. She cries out.

CAROLINE   (*Taking his spanking hand from her hip and holding it before his face.*)

Can you not.

CAROLINE *pauses. Stares transfixed at his hand.*

She retches.

BRET   Sorry I thought /

He is cut off by her violently throwing up all over him, hitting him right in the face.

Jesus Christ.

She takes a sip of water.

Oh my God.

CAROLINE   Sorr– /

She throws up again.

BRET   Fucking hell.

Still nauseous and going to be sick again she runs out the room.

So I'm polydactyl, everyone on my mum's side is, it's very normal, there's no need to be a judgemental bitch.

She slams the door.

BRET *stands and shakes off, disgusted.*

3. GRACIE & ETHEL

Kitchen.

BRET *becomes* GRACIE. *She stands before a blender covered in chicken soup* (*sick from previous scene*).

GRACIE	Oh... shit!
	ETHEL *enters.*
ETHEL	I've been doing some research.
GRACIE	I'm covered in chicken soup.
ETHEL	Bertold Wiesner
GRACIE	Ethel I'm, I'm covered in chicken soup.
ETHEL	Most prolific sperm donor of all time.
GRACIE	What?
ETHEL	(*Looking up for the first time.*)
	What happened to you?
GRACIE	Soup
ETHEL	Why's it on your face?
GRACIE	Blender! Lid! Phewf! Tell me about sperm!
ETHEL	Why was it in the blender?
GRACIE	Your mother's coming, I was making chicken soup.
ETHEL	She doesn't like it creamed.
GRACIE	Right well, that's just as well, does she like eating it off my face?
ETHEL	I'll buy the Covent Garden one from Tesco. Do you reckon three will be enough?
GRACIE	Tell me about the sperm donor.
ETHEL	If I get six she'll be more likely to believe we made it. Keep some to freeze.

GRACIE	Ethel.
ETHEL	Yes Gracie.
GRACIE	Sperm. You were talking about a sperm donor.
ETHEL	I'm doing some research.
GRACIE	Right. Is that the kind of thing you want to talk about?
ETHEL	Well, yeah. That's why I'm, that's what we're doing actually.
GRACIE	Right. Well. All Ears.
ETHEL	Okay, well, I wanted to tell you about it. Not that you. You don't at all have to be involved in this yourself. Not at all.
GRACIE	I don't need to be involved. At all.
ETHEL	No
GRACIE	You don't want me to be involved.
ETHEL	Well, no, not if you don't. No. I just thought I should tell you about it.
GRACIE	Yeah.
ETHEL	Yeah
GRACIE	Right so you're just gonna go off and do this on your own. Leave me /
ETHEL	Well yeah, it's my thing.
GRACIE	Are we breaking up right now?
ETHEL	What?! Why would... why is me finding my, why is this a big deal?
GRACIE	Why is this a big deal?
ETHEL	Yes.
GRACIE	If you don't know that then I absolutely don't think you are ready to do this.

ETHEL	Is this about *your* dad. I'm sorry. I know, it's not a great time to… It must be. I want to. I want to.
	And the last thing I want to do to you is 'find my family' just as you… lose. What am I saying. This feels like something I need to do.
GRACIE	You finding *your* family?
ETHEL	Well yeah. That's how I feel [about it].
GRACIE	I thought I was your family.
ETHEL	Yeah but not like… I just. I really think it might be him. I've got this feeling. It's him.
GRACIE	Who?
ETHEL	Bertold Wiesner.
GRACIE;	Who's Bertold Wiesner?
ETHEL	The sperm donor.
GRACIE	You've already found him.
ETHEL	Yeah.
GRACIE	And you're gonna…
ETHEL	Yeah… he's dead but
GRACIE	He's dead!?
ETHEL	Yes.
GRACIE	Why is he dead?
ETHEL	Well because he died.
GRACIE	Is that legal?
ETHEL	Well they can't exactly punish you for it can they.
GRACIE	How do you even take a sample from a corpse?
ETHEL	Well he has a son, who, can /

GRACIE   I don't understand any of this.

ETHEL   I want to know where I Come From!

You've got soup on your nose.

ETHEL tries to wipe the soup off of GRACIE's *nose.*

She flinches away.

ETHEL *tries again.*

GRACIE *grabs the tea towel from her and cleans herself.*

She makes a show of hitting the soup off, thumbing her nose at ETHEL.

She sits in a huff and becomes KIERAN. ETHEL *becomes* RITA.

4. KIERAN & RITA

KIERAN	Your nose looks like mine.
RITA	No
KIERAN	It does.
RITA	Does it?
KIERAN	It does.
RITA	I think it's in the chin.
KIERAN	I've a weaker chin than you I think.
RITA	You don't.
KIERAN	I do.
RITA	Eyes are. Different.
KIERAN	But also the same.
RITA	Yes also the same.
KIERAN	Funny.
RITA	It's not so much a feature I think. It's not a feature that we have the same. But a look.
KIERAN	Same face different features.
RITA	Exactly.
KIERAN	We look. Related.
RITA	Yes.
KIERAN	We talk the same too.
RITA	Yes.
KIERAN	Do you think so?
RITA	Over email certainly.
KIERAN	Oh yes certainly over email.
BOTH	Like I was emailing myself. Yes.
RITA	Shall we do this then?

KIERAN	Yeah.
RITA	I'm nervous.
KIERAN	Me too.
RITA	Why is it important?
KIERAN	I don't know.
RITA	Why is it important?
KIERAN	I don't know.
RITA	I don't know.
KIERAN	But it is.
RITA	It is.
KIERAN	It really is.
RITA	Okay.
KIERAN	Ready?
RITA	Yes.
KIERAN	Okay.
RITA	Okay.
KIERAN	Open wide.
RITA	Should I close my eyes?
KIERAN	No. Well. If you want to. You don't have to.
RITA	I think I want to.
KIERAN	Okay.

RITA *squeezes her eyes shut and opens her mouth.* KIERAN *inserts a cotton-wool bud and scratches.*

Rub vigorously for five, four, three,

RITA *retches.*

two,

Still rubbing.

You alright?

RITA *retches a bit more and gives him a thumbs-up.*

one.

Done.

You okay there?

RITA	Sensitive gag reflex. I'll be fine.

Do I do you?

KIERAN	I've done me.
RITA	What happens now?
KIERAN	Takes about a month.
RITA	Okay.
KIERAN	Okay.
RITA	This could be…
KIERAN	It might not be.
RITA	No. But it could be.
KIERAN	It could be.

RITA *retches a little more.*

KIERAN *casts around for something to help.*

RITA *retches more and becomes* CAROLINE.

KIERAN *stiffens and watches with growing repugnance, as he becomes* GRACIE.

5. GRACIE & CAROLINE

Hospital.

CAROLINE *throws up in a bin.*

GRACIE *enters.*

CAROLINE – *breezy and nonchalant – refocuses.*

CAROLINE	He seems better I think.
GRACIE	He's on cloud nine
CAROLINE	Well that's… better… isn't it? Less angry. You know. Less shouting.
	He's quite jolly like this. Isn't he?
GRACIE	If you're looking for me to congratulate you on drugging my father into oblivion /
CAROLINE	Huntington's is, it's very hard, for the family. Like watching someone dissolve. That's what one woman said. It's.
	He's in less pain now, I can assure you.
GRACIE	I don't want him to be in less pain I want him to feel every wretched cell in his body disintegrate.
CAROLINE	You don't mean that love.
GRACIE	Do I not nurse.
CAROLINE	Miller.
GRACIE	You make hats too?
CAROLINE	I'm sorry?
GRACIE	A miller
CAROLINE	Do you mean a milliner?
GRACIE	I've no idea and no interest. I'm finding you almost as insufferable as him. I presume you have a full life of equally meagre people who humour you into thinking you're quite charming but Nurse Milliner I'm never going to be one of them.

CAROLINE	I don't. Actually.
GRACIE	Well there's a shame.
CAROLINE	I went on a date. A couple of weeks. Months. Ago.
GRACIE	Congratulations.
CAROLINE	Bret.
GRACIE	And that's a name now?
CAROLINE	I sicked on him.
GRACIE	–
CAROLINE	I shouldn't have said that.
GRACIE	No.
CAROLINE	It was out of place.
GRACIE	Yes.
CAROLINE	He had six fingers.
GRACIE	Good for him.
CAROLINE	You don't see that every day.
GRACIE	No.
CAROLINE	Would you like a tea?
GRACIE	No.
CAROLINE	Coffee?
GRACIE	I'm fine.
CAROLINE	Right well I'm just going to go anyway.
GRACIE	That's fine.
CAROLINE	Just over there.
GRACIE	Okay.
CAROLINE	So if you did want /
GRACIE	I won't.
	–
	You've not gone.

CAROLINE	No.
GRACIE	Is this some kind of game?
CAROLINE	No.
GRACIE	I'm not going to report you if that's what you're worried about?
CAROLINE	What?
GRACIE	For the… 'sicking'.
CAROLINE	Oh.
GRACIE	Insubordination.
CAROLINE	Right.
GRACIE	Drunkenne– /
CAROLINE	I'm not, actually, I'm, I wouldn't
GRACIE	Well whatever. I'm not /
CAROLINE	Okay. Thanks. Thank you.
GRACIE	So you really can leave.
CAROLINE	–
GRACIE	Are you password-operated or something?
CAROLINE	You can go in you know.
GRACIE	I'm sorry?
CAROLINE	You come here every day. Stand at the window. Look through the window. Hours. You can go in you know.
	Beat.
GRACIE	Yes well.
CAROLINE	I can come in with you if you'd like.
GRACIE	Really.
CAROLINE	If you'd like.
	Beat.
GRACIE	No that's okay. I better. I better. Go on my own.

6. KIERAN & RITA

RITA	I didn't want to do it on my own.
KIERAN	So you don't [know yet].
RITA	I've got them here.
KIERAN	In there.
RITA	In here.
KIERAN	Well.
RITA	So, what's it, what's it going to tell me? What if I don't, understand it? I was looking online at gene types and it was just a long alphabet of nonsense, I couldn't make head nor tail of it.
KIERAN	No no, it's really clear, they've worked it all out for you. It will either say, you're Bertold's daughter, my sister, or that you're Richter's daughter, or that you're mystery donor C's daughter, in any of those cases I can put you in touch with some half-siblings. Or it might say that you're from someone else entirely. In which case I can help you keep looking.
RITA	I just want to say. Even if it's not a match
KIERAN	It's fine.
RITA	Even if it's not. I still, I'm really.
KIERAN	It's fine.
RITA	I'm really pleased that I met you.
KIERAN	Me too. Whatever that says, we are bonded, through this. Barton Brood. Whatever your genes are. Whoever your father is. Okay.
RITA	You've done this before.
KIERAN	What?
RITA	You're good at it.
KIERAN	Am I?

RITA	You are.
KIERAN	I am?
RITA	Very calming.
KIERAN	Thanks.

She goes to open the letter and retracts her hand.

RITA	Tell me about before.
KIERAN	What? About me?
RITA	Tell me about when you've done this before.
KIERAN	With someone else?
RITA	Yeah.
KIERAN	Okay.

–

RITA	Who's been the most shocked?
KIERAN	Ha.
RITA	No don't tell me. No go on tell me. No you don't / have to /
KIERAN	Bret. /
RITA	Who?
KIERAN	Bret. Funny guy.
RITA	American?
KIERAN	No.
RITA	Funny ha ha.
KIERAN	If you like that kind of thing…
RITA	Right.
KIERAN	He asked me what the Jewish paedophile said.
RITA	Oh.
KIERAN	Yes.

RITA	Well go on.
KIERAN	Oh, I didn't find out.
RITA	?
KIERAN	You meant the story. Not the joke.
RITA	I did.
KIERAN	Bret's father, Leopold, was very close with Mary and Bertold. Physicist. Very tall. Very handsome. Very clever.
RITA	Very good sperm.
KIERAN	Well, that's what I thought. Could he be our, mystery donor C, or D?
RITA	(*Touching her letter.*) Yes.
KIERAN	Leopold's dead.
RITA	Obviously.
KIERAN	But I find his son.
RITA	Bret
KIERAN	Yeah.
RITA	The anti-Semite.
KIERAN	And he gives me a DNA sample.
RITA	That must be weird. Must be even weirder, for them you know, being the proper child of one of those men and finding out you've a load of /
KIERAN	Oh. No. Bret had no problem with that, he was quite excited, adored his father. Said he had top genes. He doesn't want kids himself but he wants that legacy out there.
RITA	This Bret thinks a lot of himself.
KIERAN	Well he did. Bret's DNA. It proved a match alright but, not quite what we expected. Bret proved a match for Wiesner!

RITA	What?
KIERAN	Yeah.
RITA	So he's…
KIERAN	Yeah.
RITA	He was donor conceived. Not his father's at all. And he never knew?
KIERAN	Nope.
RITA	You're joking.
KIERAN	Quite a way to find out.
RITA	Yes.
KIERAN	I felt a bit guilty. He wasn't… thrilled. His father had only just died.
RITA	And now he has a brother.
KIERAN	Yes.
RITA	Your brother is an anti-Semitic Jew.
KIERAN	Half-brother.
RITA	Half. Yes. But that's the best you got.
KIERAN	That's. Would you open the letter?
RITA	Looking for an upgrade.
KIERAN	Would you open the letter?
RITA	Yep.
	She doesn't.
	Yep.
	She does so.
	Oh.
KIERAN	It's fine.
	Oh please don't cry.

RITA   Here

                        KIERAN *reads the letter. They are clearly*
                        a match. He breathes in. Hugs her.

                        They break apart as RITA *becomes* SOPHIE
                        and KIERAN *becomes* JAMES.

                        SOPHIE *holds* JAMES *at arm's length,*
                        alarmed.

7. SOPHIE & JAMES

SOPHIE   I'm so sorry.

JAMES   It's not a problem. (*It's clearly a problem.*)

SOPHIE   I thought you were [my brother].

JAMES   It's fine. (*It's awkward.*)

SOPHIE   He's [dead].

JAMES   I've got one of those faces.

                JAMES *leaves.*

                SOPHIE *crumples, embarrassed and
                heartbroken, she becomes* CAROLINE.

                JAMES, *having left, responds to an unheard
                calling back by* CAROLINE.

8. BRET & CAROLINE

BRET   What?

CAROLINE

BRET   Did.

CAROLINE   Yeah.

BRET   And.

CAROLINE   Yep.

BRET   Right.

                Right.

CAROLINE   You don't. I just thought I should. Thought
                you should.

BRET   Of course.

                Sensible girl.

CAROLINE   You don't. I just thought.

BRET   Caroline I think we should get married.

CAROLINE   What.

BRET   I think that you should be my wife. Will you
                agree to be my wife.

CAROLINE   Um.

BRET   I really think it would be best.

CAROLINE   Okay.

BRET   Okay marvellous. Oh god I really do have to.
                I'm late.

CAROLINE   That's okay. Me too actually.

BRET   No it's really not I'm never late. I'll call you.

CAROLINE   Okay.

BRET   Okay.

CAROLINE   Okay.

BRET   Okay.

They have the awkwardest kiss known to man.

Depart.

Return.

CAROLINE   Sorry I'm actually going that way.

BRET   That's. Bye.

CAROLINE   Bye.

                       CAROLINE *busies off and* BRET *sits
                       stunned. Tries to collect himself.*

                       He falls in on himself and becomes GRACIE.

9. ETHEL & GRACIE

ETHEL   Hello lamb.

GRACIE   –

ETHEL   You still not talking to me?

GRACIE   –

ETHEL   You gonna tell me why you're not talking
               to me?

GRACIE   I'm embarrassed.

ETHEL   Why are you embarrassed?

GRACIE   –

ETHEL   Gracie?

GRACIE   Because I got really cross and angry over a
               misunderstanding that I'm now a hundred per
               cent sure that I was wrong about but I'm still
               chemically quite enraged and not prepared to
               climb down and I'm also just really sad and
               my father's dying and I don't really have the
               emotional space to countenance us not getting
               on right now and I know I really should be the
               one apologising but I absolutely don't feel in
               the mood to do that and so I think it's
               probably best if I just stay silent.

ETHEL   You wanna stay silent in company?

               GRACIE *shrugs*.

               ETHEL *curls into her.*

GRACIE   So you don't want a baby then?

ETHEL   Well.

               She strokes GRACIE*'s hair.*

               At the moment. I've already got one.

               She kisses GRACIE*'s forehead.*

               Tender.

GRACIE   Whah.

                (*Purposefully creepy.*)

                Can I have some milk please Mummy.

                ETHEL *pushes her off the sofa.*

                GRACIE *recovers herself and sits as* BRET.

                Speaks to an unseen waiter.

10. RITA & BRET

Café.

BRET	No milk. Just black.
RITA	What do you call those big white tents? (Frappuccino please.)
BRET	Marquees
RITA	Yes. (Extra shot.) We'll have one of those. (Ooh. And some syrup. Caramel. Yes. And a hot cheesy croissant. No tomato.) ((I can't stand tomato.)) We'll have a Marquee we'll fill it to the brim. Fill it to the brim with new family.
BRET	Like a wedding
RITA	Like a wedding. Exactly.
BRET	You seem. Enthused.
RITA	Well it's exciting isn't it?
BRET	I'm getting married.
RITA	Congratulations.
BRET	Thank you.
RITA	You should invite us all! No, no I shouldn't have said that.
BRET	Well it's tomorrow so…
RITA	I'm free. That's not what you meant. Sorry, I'm excited. You're only the third I've met.
BRET	Oh well, you're ahead of me there. You're my second, only Kieran.
RITA	Lovely Kieran. Lynchpin Kieran.
	But there's plenty more.
BRET	So I hear.
RITA	I feel so razzed.

BRET   Razzed?

RITA   Razzed it means – (*Thinks.*) Jazzed

BRET   I don't think it does.

RITA   It's American I think.

BRET   Right.

RITA   (*Holds her stomach.*)

            (Do you know I'm not sure I need another coffee.)

            You don't seem very happy.

BRET   About my wedding? No.

RITA   Oh. I meant about this. Oh.

BRET   Cattle are bred this way you know. For meat. Hundreds at a time. Just like us.

RITA   We were planned.

BRET   What.

            BRET *stands.*

RITA   Planned. How many people can say that? Fewer than you think.

BRET   (*Thinks.*) That. Is certainly true.

            BRET *disappears into himself.*

            RITA *holds her stomach.*

            She becomes CAROLINE.

11. CAROLINE & KIERAN

CAROLINE *is at her nurses' station talking to her stomach.*

CAROLINE   Matilda told such dreadful lies, it made one
             gasp and stretch one's / (*Jumps.*) Visiting
             hours are over I'm afraid.

KIERAN   Are they? Damn.

CAROLINE   Who. Um. Who were you here to see?

KIERAN   Caroline Miller.

CAROLINE   Oh, right. Uh, Caroline Miller?

KIERAN   I was told she was here.

CAROLINE   Yes.

KIERAN   God she's not dead is she?

CAROLINE   Ha ha. No love, she's not dead.

KIERAN   Good

CAROLINE   She's Caroline Bretton now though. Is there
             anything you wanted her for. Specifically?

KIERAN   She's my sister.

CAROLINE   Your sister?

KIERAN   My sister yes. My whole sister. Only, she
             doesn't know. Damn. I don't know why I told
             you. Forget that I told you. Is she. So she's
             not dead.

CAROLINE   She's not dead no.

KIERAN   And I really can't see her. Even though she's
             my sister. And I've never met her. Which
             you've forgotten that I told you. So that's.
             Yep. What is it about uniforms, you tell
             people things when they're wearing a uniform
             don't you. People tell people who are wearing
             uniforms things that they don't tell other
             people. Do you get that a lot? I've never had
             a uniform. Except at school. No one told you
             anything then, but that's different I suppose

isn't it. 'Cept Maths. Of course. I was never
very good at maths. Better at biology. School
uniform. God I'm nervous can you tell.

CAROLINE   I think we better have a cup of tea love.

KIERAN   Oh god she is dead isn't she?

            KIERAN *becomes* GRACIE *and* CAROLINE
            becomes ETHEL.

12. ETHEL & GRACIE

ETHEL	No. Really. (Shall we get a takeaway?)
GRACIE	Mary Barton. Yeah. (Yes.)
ETHEL	Yeah
GRACIE	I've heard of her
ETHEL	Actually? (Do you want Chinese or Indian?)
GRACIE	Yeah. My father hated her. (Chinese I think.) Hated her.
ETHEL	Why?
GRACIE	He was mates with um... um... Lord Blackford.
ETHEL	Crispy duck and a mixed hors d'oeuvres?
GRACIE	Put her up in front of Parliament. (Yeah and an extra prawn toast.)
ETHEL	Why?
GRACIE	They're always really tiddly the starter ones, dry.
ETHEL	–
GRACIE	Adultery isn't it. Using another man's sperm.
ETHEL	No. (Amazing you can do this online now isn't it?)
GRACIE	Hardly a traditional family union is it?
ETHEL	Well nor are we.
GRACIE	No, he'd hate you too.
ETHEL	Yes I gathered that from you introducing me as your cleaner.
GRACIE	You ever gonna let that go?
ETHEL	Probably not.
	Hey if your father hates her so much, maybe you're a Barton Brooder too.

GRACIE	Ha, we could be sisters, that would be funny.
ETHEL	Sure, funny in a, 'ha ha my life is over' kind of way.
GRACIE	You're so hilariously dramatic.
ETHEL	It would be a disaster.
GRACIE	You just don't want me chumming up to your new mates.
ETHEL	No, I would be devastated that I'd lost the love of my life.
GRACIE	Lost how?
ETHEL	We would be sisters, we would have to break up immediately and spend the rest of our lives in therapy.
GRACIE	Of course we wouldn't, what difference would it make, we just wouldn't tell anyone.
ETHEL	Can you hear what you're saying?
GRACIE	I can't believe that you would leave me.
ETHEL	What did I do? Where are you going?
GRACIE	Out. To see my actual father and escape this hypothetical nightmare where you're a complete wanker.

ETHEL *is alone a moment. As* REBECCA *enters, busy,* ETHEL *becomes* SUZIE.

13. REBECCA & SUZIE

REBECCA   At work this afternoon, Charles, from
                 accounts, asked me for a drink

SUZIE   Ooh. Is he handsome?

REBECCA   No. Charles said. 'Do you want a drink?' And
                 I said 'No I can't tonight. My sister's coming
                 to stay.'

SUZIE   Ha!

REBECCA   And he didn't bat an eyelid. Well why would
                 he? Why should he? I've just. I've never been
                 able to say that before.

SUZIE   No. No me neither.

REBECCA   It's nice

SUZIE   It Is nice.

                 REBECCA *becomes* KIERAN *and* SUZIE
                 becomes CAROLINE.

                 The dynamic is the opposite.

                 Where REBECCA *and* SUZIE *have found*
                 warmth, KIERAN *and* CAROLINE *have*
                 found only awkwardness.

14. CAROLINE & KIERAN

Graveyard.

KIERAN	Bit morbid. Having a graveyard next to a hospital.
CAROLINE	Saves on transportation.
KIERAN	Yes. I imagine.
CAROLINE	It. Was a joke.
KIERAN	Of course.
CAROLINE	Sorry.
KIERAN	Please. Don't apologise. I like jokes.
CAROLINE	Okay.
KIERAN	I like jokes.
CAROLINE	That's lucky.
KIERAN	I make jokes.
CAROLINE	Even better.
KIERAN	I'm just. I'm just…
CAROLINE	Nervous.
KIERAN	Nervous. Yes. This is really the hardest time that I've done this. And the best, as well, I hope the best. I'm so nervous. I don't usually get nervous. Usually I'm /
CAROLINE	How many times have you done this?
KIERAN	Well, never quite this, but, a lot.
	–
CAROLINE	It's November the first today.
KIERAN	It is.
CAROLINE	All Saints' Day.
KIERAN	Yes.

CAROLINE   You know if we were in Poland this graveyard
                would be full. First of November, covered in
                candles and picnics and people.

                Eating and talking and laughing and telling
                stories about the dead. In a happy way.

KIERAN   That sounds nice.

CAROLINE   It was nice. I went once when I was small.
                We wanted to join in. We looked for miles for
                an unattended grave, but there wasn't one.

KIERAN   I'm gonna be cremated. Let no one witness
                the dissolution of my memory.

CAROLINE   Do you want to? Find one. Tidy it up a bit.
                Play at being family.

                Of the dead people.

                Family of the dead people.

KIERAN   I have an egg sandwich. We could reward
                ourselves.

CAROLINE   That'd be nice.

KIERAN   So, who do you want then? Creepy crying
                angel with the empty Glen's vodka and
                Burger King?

CAROLINE   Someone had a party.

KIERAN   Not as much as war memorial over there.
                Is that a condom? Who has sex on a grave?

CAROLINE   Maybe they were trying to reincarnate
                someone.

KIERAN   With a condom?

CAROLINE   –

                Maud Gonne.

KIERAN   Hm?

CAROLINE   Had sex. On her son's grave.

KIERAN	That's quite a kink.
CAROLINE	With her estranged husband.
KIERAN	Did it work? Did she… reincarnate him?
CAROLINE	(*Raises her eyebrows.*)
	Well she had a baby.
KIERAN	And…?
CAROLINE	It was a girl.
KIERAN	Ah.
CAROLINE	Iseult.
KIERAN	Iseult. You can tell she was disappointed.
CAROLINE	I think it's pretty. But you might be right. Maud told everyone Iseult was her cousin.
KIERAN	That makes me so angry. Poor Iseult. It's not her fault she wasn't born a boy. Maud literally orchestrated her birth, it is entirely on her if she's disappointed by what comes out.
CAROLINE	Probably better though. Than being raised as someone you're not. Your parent, willing every inch of you to be something else.
KIERAN	I'd not thought of that. I'd not thought of that at all.
CAROLINE	So I'm your sister?
KIERAN	(*Nods.*)
CAROLINE	How's that work?
KIERAN	You were conceived through donor insemination.
CAROLINE	Was I?
	KIERAN *nods.*
	How do you know?

KIERAN   This must be a shock. I shouldn't have.

CAROLINE   I'm okay.

KIERAN   I've sprung all this on you.

CAROLINE   Just. Tell me.

KIERAN   –

                (*Goes to speak.*)

                You were conceived in a London Fertility
                Clinic run by Mary Barton and her husband
                Bertold Wiesner. They advised complete
                secrecy.

CAROLINE   Seems fair.

                KIERAN *doesn't think so.*

KIERAN   They tried really hard to prepare parents. And
                only select the ones where they thought it
                would work out. Psychologically. But they
                made some mistakes.

                They were really worried about men changing
                their minds and disowning their children.
                They only let cases go ahead if they could
                ensure 'mutual confidence' in the decision.

CAROLINE   Okay

KIERAN   But it's all sort of mind-reading.

CAROLINE   Right.

KIERAN   Basically, if the husband put his name on the
                birth certificate then the child would be
                legitimate, even though that was technically
                illegal.

CAROLINE   But how does this relate to me? I'm not
                illegitimate. I had a father.

KIERAN   When Beatrice Miller, had her, artificial
                insemination.

She – eh, became pregnant with twins. And when they were born, there was a girl, you. and a boy.

Her husband. Samuel Miller. Accepted the girl and signed her birth certificate. But he rejected the boy. A sort of compromise.

CAROLINE   And I never knew.

KIERAN   He didn't want his name carried on by a child that wasn't genetically his. Well you see, a girl would take her husband's name. But a boy, a boy would keep his.

CAROLINE   So?

KIERAN   Legacy is important to some people.

CAROLINE   You mean men.

KIERAN   Some men.

CAROLINE *becomes* MARCUS, KIERAN *becomes* KEITH.

15. MARCUS & KEITH

Pub.

MARCUS   You're going double-barrelled?

KEITH   Yeah.

MARCUS   Are you a wanker?

KEITH   No, Kim wants her (phone away, pub time)
                Kim wants her name in too, and so

MARCUS   You've become a wanker.

KEITH   No. (Seriously it's the quiz tonight, if
                Martin /)

MARCUS   You've got something on your face.

KEITH   That's just my face.

MARCUS   No honestly you've got. Oh no it Is attached.
                (Lisa's coming.)

KEITH   Put the phone away.

MARCUS   Yeah.

                MARCUS *becomes* ETHEL. KEITH *becomes*
                GRACIE. *It's sobering.*

16. ETHEL & GRACIE

GRACIE	Put the laptop away.
ETHEL	Yep.
GRACIE	Put the laptop away now.
ETHEL	Two minutes.
GRACIE	It's our anniversary.
ETHEL	And it will still be our anniversary in two minutes.
GRACIE	Ethel. Ethel. This is important to me Ethel.
ETHEL	Don't use my name Gracie, I hate it when you do that.
GRACIE	Okay. Cyber-obsessed, unromantic wanker.
	GRACIE *slams closed the laptop*.
ETHEL	Jesus Christ Gracie, I'm just saying goodbye.
GRACIE	It's our anniversary.
ETHEL	Which you've ruined.
GRACIE	What?
ETHEL	If you'd have waited. Two minutes. It would have been fine. Now Suzie is asking me what's wrong and I'm going to have to explain.
GRACIE	Who the fuck is Suzie and why do you have to explain anything to her.
ETHEL	Suzie is my sister, you know this.
GRACIE	She's not your sister. You've never met her. You don't even know her.
ETHEL	That's a really horrible thing to say. And I do know her actually. We IM. She's sixty-nine, lives in Gloucester, is a retired paediatricia– /
GRACIE	I don't need a fact file. Your life was entirely complete before you started with this mad obsession. You're shutting me out.

ETHEL   I'm shutting you out?! You won't even let me
            come to the fucking hospital with you. You
            ignore every conversation I try and start about
            your dad. I'm trying to be there for you
            Gracie but you make it really hard. Really,
            really hard.

GRACIE   You didn't even know, the password, to that
            laptop, three weeks ago. It's my laptop.

ETHEL   Okay, so I'll buy a laptop.

GRACIE   I don't I don't want you to buy a laptop.

17. BRET & CAROLINE

They are shopping for baby clothes.

CAROLINE	Everything yellow, it's so, so… what's the word
BRET	Yellow?
CAROLINE	Impersonal yellow. Don't you think?
BRET	I've not thought no.
CAROLINE	I just want little poppet to feel like we know them, you know. Yellow's well, not the colour of something you buy for someone you know, you know?
BRET	I'm not sure I do.
CAROLINE	Well. You're a man. Maybe poppet's a man and he won't mind so much.
BRET	Caroline.
CAROLINE	Would you rather a boy? Or a girl?
BRET	Caroline, Caroline please we really need to sit down somewhere, and go and talk.
CAROLINE	No time. There's no time, darling.
BRET	We've got to make time. Now, right now, let's go. Get a coffee /
CAROLINE	You know I can't have caffeine.
BRET	A decaf.
CAROLINE	Oh no, I don't like decaf. You can just tell, it's got an emptiness to it, do you know what I mean?
BRET	A hot chocolate then, the drink is really not what's important.
CAROLINE	I'm trying to cut down on sugar.
BRET	Please, my / Caroline. It's – (*Almost tearing up.*) we really need to /

CAROLINE   Honey, I'm saving all my maternity for once
             poppet is born, I'm working all the hours until
             then, Sundays need to be for shopping, we
             need everything ready. Now whatever it is,
             just say it.

BRET   –

CAROLINE   I'm your wife. You can say anything to me.
             Go on.

BRET   –

CAROLINE   Whatever it is, me and poppet are here for
             you.

BRET   You're going to have to get an abortion.

             –

             I'm so sorry. I'm so so sorry Caroline. This is
             such a horrible mess.

CAROLINE   What?

BRET   I'm sorry. I'm just sorry. I don't know what
             else to say.

CAROLINE   But, I'm... twenty weeks. Poppet's a person.
             What's. Why would you... This is all I've
             ever wanted.

             CAROLINE *is crying.*

BRET   Listen. I don't know how to say this. This, is
             hard for me too.

CAROLINE   But we're married and we're having a baby.

BRET   I

CAROLINE   We're the perfect family. We've made the
             perfect family.

BRET   I saw you in the graveyard with Kieran.

CAROLINE   It's really not what you think.

BRET   Caroline I'm so sorry but you have to
             understand.

CAROLINE	I share an egg sandwich with another man you're insisting I get an abortion?
BRET	Caroline.
CAROLINE	He's my brother Bret. He's my brother.
BRET	Yes. Yes, I know.
CAROLINE	So what the problem?
BRET	He's my brother too.
CAROLINE	What are you talking about?
BRET	He's my brother, Caroline. He found me. You're my sister. Our wedding is illegitimate. That fetus is inbred. You're going to have to get an abortion.
CAROLINE	Oow.
	Jesus.
BRET	God what a mess. What a fucking mess. (*Hits something.*)
CAROLINE	Right. Okay. Right.
	Right.
	Okay.
	Look. I'm going to tell you something now, Bret, and I need you to focus very, very, hard on the positives. And not the negatives okay.
BRET	I'm really struggling to see a positive at all /
CAROLINE	And I'm going to help you with that.
BRET	I'm really struggling Caroline to think of a thing that you might say that could possibly make this better right now.
CAROLINE	It's not yours.
BRET	I'm sorry what?
CAROLINE	It's not yours.

BRET	It's not mine?
CAROLINE	Yes.
BRET	So, you're telling me that not only is my wife my sister but she's also a fucking whore.
CAROLINE	No, I see how you think that. But I'm not a whore.
BRET	You're a whore Caroline. A whore. You sleep with another man and expect me to raise his baby
CAROLINE	No. No see that's the magic of it.
BRET	The magic?
CAROLINE	I was artificially inseminated see.
BRET	We had a shotgun wedding Caroline because /
CAROLINE	Because we love each other.
BRET	Because you were pregnant.
CAROLINE	No see, I actually had had the insemination, just that second, just that minute when I met you.
	I came out. Of my procedure, and you were there. Two gifts. From God. We had this… affinity
BRET	That might be Caroline because we're fucking related.
CAROLINE	Yes. Yes, maybe it was. But it doesn't really matter how it started. We're here now and isn't it perfect.
BRET	You're insane Caroline.
CAROLINE	Oh I'm not lying darling. Do you remember when I was poorly on you the first time we made love. That was morning sickness…
BRET	You just said it was the same day. How can you have morning sickness, the same day?

CAROLINE   It was a sign! Look it is perfect see, because
             we'll never be able to have a proper baby
             together. It might be. Deformed. But this way
             we can be a happy family, with a baby and no
             one need ever know.

BRET   That's disgusting.

CAROLINE   We'll need to be really careful. I'll get the
             pill. Or we can not have sex. If you like. Lots
             of marriages are sexless aren't they. In the
             end. It's perfect. And look, think, we both
             grew up not knowing our father wasn't our
             father and that was completely fine, wasn't it.
             Completely fine. We'd never have known if it
             hadn't been for stupid Kieran. Stupid Kieran
             and his bag of worms.

BRET   You're Touched. You're medically deranged.

CAROLINE   Can of worms, I meant can of worms. We can
             make this work darling.

BRET   Caroline. I never want to see you. In my life.
             Ever again.

             BRET *storms off.*

             CAROLINE *paces. Anxious. At breaking
             point. She becomes* ETHEL. *Equally nervy.*

18. ETHEL & VENTRILOQUIST

VENTRILOQUIST (*puppet*)

    Turn that frown upside down missy.

ETHEL   Sorry, I just needed some – (*Noticing the puppet*.) air

VENTRILOQUIST (*puppet*)

    No point in breathing the air if it don't make you happy.

ETHEL   This is a hospital car park; not a theme park.

VENTRILOQUIST (*puppet*)

    Oh I know that, I know that well, my father here, lost his wife in that very building, floor three, cancer it was, of the lung. He don't say much these days so now I do the talking for both of us, he just sits, smokes, waits for his life to fade away. I can't breathe myself but if I could I'd be sure to make every gulp of it into a smile. Life's too short to waste on frowns.

ETHEL   I'm sorry that your wife died.

    Puppet turns his head to the
    VENTRILOQUIST.

VENTRILOQUIST (*puppet*)

    You'll be lucky to get a word out of him. I've been trying all day.

ETHEL   Could I have a cigarette please?

VENTRILOQUIST (*puppet*)

    Oh they're very bad for you lady, hey don't you go giving her one of those.

    VENTRILOQUIST *hands her a cigarette*.

ETHEL   Thank you.

VENTRILOQUIST (*puppet*)

    Nasty tar you're poisoning up your throat there. Mm benzene. Love benzene.

ETHEL   Could you please shut up.

VENTRILOQUIST (*puppet*)
      Rude she is too.

ETHEL   I'm sitting on a bench, smoking a cigarette,
      stalking the person I love and talking to a
      crazy person. Am I somehow fourteen again?

VENTRILOQUIST (*puppet*)
      Oh he's not crazy.

ETHEL   Please.

VENTRILOQUIST (*himself*)
      He's a bit [crazy].

      You got someone in there.

ETHEL   Uh... yeah. I think so. Won't talk to me.

VENTRILOQUIST (*himself*)
      Losing the love of your life is worse than
      losing your life I think. I envy her that. I'd
      give everything I own, for one more bitter,
      cruel, mad fight with my Iris.

      Long beat.

ETHEL   I'm sorry. I.

      Long beat.

VENTRILOQUIST (*himself*)
      Go and speak to him.

      Do whatever he wants.

      While you've got the chance.

      You'll regret it if you don't.

ETHEL   Right.

      Right.

      They sit a while. Smoking.

      Yeah.

      Oh uh.

      She wants to throw her butt away.

VENTRILOQUIST (*himself*)

>   (*Opens the mouth of the* PUPPET.)

>   Stick it in there.

VENTRILOQUIST (*puppet*)
>   Oh no, please missus. Please.

VENTRILOQUIST (*himself*)
>   Go on, he's only teasing.

>   *She goes to.*

VENTRILOQUIST (*puppet*)
>   Please. Please. Agh. I can't bear it.

>   *She hesitates.*

VENTRILOQUIST (*himself*)
>   He can't actually feel anything he is a puppet.

VENTRILOQUIST (*puppet*)
>   Agghh

>   *She does.*

>   Agghh. Horrid horrid lady.

>   *She smiles. Strokes the puppet.*

>   *The* VENTRILOQUIST *draws the puppet away from her and lies him out on the bench which becomes a bed.*

>   ETHEL *gives them some space.*

>   *The* VENTRILOQUIST *draws a sheet up over the puppet. Stares at it. Becomes* GRACIE.

19. CAROLINE & GRACIE

Hospital.

CAROLINE   How you doing?

GRACIE   It's quiet.

CAROLINE   It's late.

GRACIE   'Silent as the grave'

CAROLINE   Yes.

GRACIE   It's been so busy, so many people, that I've never met. Never met.

CAROLINE   I can give you a little longer but I'm here to tell you if we want to be in time to use any of his organs we should get him to the morgue quite quickly.

GRACIE   Using his…?

CAROLINE   He was on the donor list.

GRACIE   I didn't know.

CAROLINE   As I say if you'd like a little longer…

GRACIE   Quite like the idea of him living on in someone else.

CAROLINE   That can be a comfort

GRACIE   Takes the pressure off. Me.

CAROLINE   Right

GRACIE   I'm all that's left of him that's living and there's not a grain of me I feel is a part of him.

CAROLINE   You weren't close?

GRACIE   We were too close. Locked in a life together.

              When I was four my mother drove us to Dover with a suitcase. It was blue.

              She bought tickets for a boat. He came after us. He was livid.

He didn't like her to drive at night.

She said we'd been to see her mother and got lost on the way back. My grandmother lived in Sussex and we in London so it was pretty lost.

They put Mum on some medication after that. She died a few years later. Hit by a car.

The drugs made her a little – floaty.

Sometimes I think about my life as a French woman with a live mother and blue suitcase to remember this one.

CAROLINE   Life as a single mother would have been very hard.

GRACIE   Very hard. But better.

CAROLINE   Very hard. But maybe better.

GRACIE   You can take him.

CAROLINE   Who?

GRACIE   My father. To the

CAROLINE   Morgue.

GRACIE   To the morgue.

20. JAMES & BRET

JAMES   How does that make you feel?

BRET   Pretty Confused.

21. KIERAN & RITA

KIERAN	She won't return my calls. I spent so long, trying to find her, and we had this, connection, and, now she just won't call me back.
RITA	Some people don't want to be found.
KIERAN	That's easy for you to say. You've got four children, and about a million grandchildren and they love you. She's my sister and I don't have anyone else.
RITA	You've got us lot. 'The Found.' The Barton Brood.
KIERAN	And what about the nine hundred of us that will never know. What about them? They're just existing out there not even knowing that they're our brother, or sister.
RITA	(*Studies him.*) It's been quite a year for you Kieran. Losing your mother.
KIERAN	Karen wasn't my mother.
RITA	Of course she was my love. Of course she was.
KIERAN	Beatrice Miller was my mother and she left me and now Caroline is leaving me all over again.
RITA	I'm going to tell you something Kieran but after I have I don't want to talk about it now or ever again is that okay.
KIERAN	Okay.
RITA	When I was sixteen it was the Late Fifties. Hippies didn't exist yet but if they had I would have been one. My mother still bought all of my clothes and they were pretty drab but I used to decorate myself with flowers from the garden. I looked quite mad. One day, and it must have been spring because the cherry blossoms were out. (I had stripped this poor

tree bare.) ((I used to have this mane of hair down to here and I'd woven every inch of it with blossom.)) There was a scarecrow festival in the next village, and I tell you I could have passed for one of them. Anyway, I had missed my lift and was walking very rigidly, like this, so as not to let any of the petals fall out of my hair, and I saw a man coming towards me who I had never seen before, and have never seen again in fact. His name was John and he looked like a badger. He had dark hair and a pale white face with a pointy nose, and he was the best thing that I'd ever seen. He told me that I was beautiful, which I wasn't before he said it. We found a barn and we had sex. It was lovely and it didn't hurt at all at the time. I lost quite a lot of petals mind. Anyway I think you know where this is going. There were no abortions at that time. The doctor suggested gins, a hot bath, a douche. I was sent to the Catholic Crusade of Rescue. I never held my baby. I don't know if they were a boy or a girl. I've tried quite hard to find them. In these last few years especially. But I imagine they were never told. Any time I meet a doctor, or a shop assistant, with a pointy nose and black hair I do wonder. It makes me nicer to people on the whole I think. I think it makes me kinder. There is huge value to being connected to the world that way. To share a bit of life with someone, even if they don't want to be found.

–

KIERAN	I think I'll throw Caroline a baby shower. And invite all us sibs.
RITA	Oh, Kieran I'm not sure.
KIERAN	She thinks she doesn't have a family. I'll show her she does.

22. GRACIE & REGISTRAR

GRACIE *stands holding a reel of tickets from a 'take a ticket and wait' machine.*

REGISTRAR   We operate a ticketed waiting system madam and I am currently waiting on ticket holder four-two-three. You appear to be in possession of tickets four-six-seven through seven-eight-nine.

GRACIE   Please.

RESISTRAR   It's not at my discretion.

GRACIE   I can't be in that room any more. I didn't, I didn't realise it was all one building.

REGISTRAR   You must be a death. As are many people before you in the queue. From experience madam. If it's not too bold, your grief will be no worse in that room, than it will be on the Tube home, the walk to your door, or the cry you have over an overheated bowl of spaghetti hoops because you forgot to do the shopping.

GRACIE   So many babies. There are so many babies.

REGISTRAR   Birth, death and marriage. We do it all. And civil partnerships now of course. We're expanding. We'll be registering lions and tigers next.

GRACIE   Will you.

REGISTRAR   You didn't lose a child, did you?

GRACIE   No.

REGISTRAR   Well that's alright then. Go on, who were they then, might as well now you're in the room. Whose death are you here to register?

GRACIE   My father.

REGISTRAR   Very good. Do you have medical certificate stating cause of death?

GRACIE *hands across a file*.

GRACIE   Everyone in that room felt right at the
                beginning of something. You know. Life,
                parenthood, marriage.

REGISTRAR   Some people find that a comfort, when
                they've lost someone. Life goes on, you
                know.

GRACIE   They must be generous.

REGISTRAR   It'll all end in tears. Take comfort in that.

GRACIE   Sometimes I just feel, I'm in the job I'm
                going to die in, I'm in the relationship I'm
                gonna die in, I live in the house I'm gonna die
                in, am I ever gonna start a something new like
                that? Have I ever.

REGISTRAR   Well that's you all done. Thanks for dropping
                in. Now if you wouldn't mind the real four-
                two-three is waiting. Ta-ta. See you when
                your mother dies.

GRACIE   She's already dead.

REGISTRAR   Well there's a bit of good news for me. Safe
                home Grace. And try not to drink too much.
                It won't make you feel better in the long run.

                Exit GRACIE.

23. REGISTRAR & BRET

Enter BRET.

REGISTRAR   Oh good you're back.

BRET   Sorry?

REGISTRAR   Oh I'm sorry I thought you were the lady before you?

BRET   The lady?

REGISTRAR   You have the same Jizz.

BRET   Excuse me?

REGISTRAR   You have the same Jizz.

–

Jizz. You're not a birder? Jizz is the essence, the overall impression of an animal, the shadow you catch in the corner of your eye. Vibe if you will; indefinable quality. You sir have the same jizz as that lady.

Birth marriage or death sir.

BRET   Birth and marriage.

REGISTRAR   How modern of you.

BRET   I'm here to request my birth certificate, I have an alteration to make and to destroy all record of my marriage to a Miss Caroline Miller.

REGISTRAR   Oh. I see. Sir provided you were born in England or Wales you're best off registering on the General Register Office website if you want to order a copy of a birth certificate. Certificates cost nine pounds twenty-five and are sent after fourteen working days. If you need your certificate sooner you can use the priority service for twenty-three pounds forty. It will be sent the next working day if you order by 4 p.m. Whatever you wish to do with

your own copy in your own home is up to
you. If you would like to make an official
correction to your birth certificate to change
say your father's details?

BRET   –

REGISTRAR   You will need either a court order or a DNA
test to prove that your recorded father is not
your natural father.

BRET   I have DNA evidence yes, that I was donor-
conceived.

REGISTRAR   That you were donor-conceived?

BRET   Yes. Do you have a problem with that?

REGISTRAR   The problem doesn't appear to be mine sir. As
a child of donor conception myself I couldn't
imagine erasing the man who nurtured me
from the official record in favour of a stranger
who gifted me a masturbatory emission
before I was even born. But given your age
and the lack of legal definition surrounding
donor conception at your birth I imagine it's
something that you could pursue if you
wanted to.

BRET   –

REGISTRAR   Well shall we move on to your marriage and
come back to your birth at a later point.

BRET *nods*.

If you're a seeking annulment you will need
some reason to prove the marriage has always
been invalid or is defective.

BRET   Invalid and defective.

REGISTRAR   For example if the marriage wasn't
consummated?

BRET   Yep.

REGISTRAR   If you did not properly consent to the marriage.

BRET	Yep.
REGISTRAR	Because you were drunk?
BRET	Yep.
REGISTRAR	Or forced into it?
BRET	Yep.
RESIGISTRAR	If the other person had a sexually transmitted disease.
BRET	(*Shrugs*.)
REGISTRAR	If she was pregnant by another man.
BRET	Yep.
REGISTRAR	Or, if one of you is already married, either of you were under sixteen or you are closely related.
BRET	Yep.
REGISTRAR	Do any of these apply.
BRET	Quite a few yep.
REGISTRAR	Well then you certainly have grounds for an annulment. You'll have to fill out a nullity petition. They cost five hundred and fifty pounds.
BRET	Fine.
REGISTRAR	Forms can be found on our website and submitted to your nearest divorce court. Now if that's everything Mr…?
BRET	Bretton.
REGISTRAR	Now if that's everything Mr Bretton we are running over time and I have a party to get to.
	Exit BRET.

24. ETHEL & GRACIE

GRACIE	Have we got a gift?
ETHEL	What?
GRACIE	A gift. We can't go to a baby shower without a gift.
ETHEL	Oh. Babe.
GRACIE	Don't worry. I knew you'd forget. I got this.
ETHEL	What's that?
GRACIE	It's a rattle. Silver. Do you like it?
ETHEL	It's beautiful Gracie.
GRACIE	It was mine. Do you want it then?
	She shakes the rattle in ETHEL*'s face.*
	For the little sprog.
ETHEL	It's far too generous.
GRACIE	Rattle rattle. Rattle rattle rattle.
ETHEL	I didn't / (*Grabbing at the rattle and stopping* GRACIE *shaking it.*) realise. It's sibs-only. The shower. I didn't realise you wanted to come.
GRACIE	Sibs?
ETHEL	Well, there's quite a few of us, and she's only got a small flat. I'm so sorry.
GRACIE	No it's fine. Do you want it then?
ETHEL	No, no. You keep it. It's yours. I got her a nappy cake anyway.
GRACIE	I thought Suzie got her the nappy cake.
ETHEL	Well I got her another one. It's not exactly gonna stop shitting is it. I really didn't think you'd have wanted to come. I'm sorry. You've not really shown any interest in this side of /
GRACIE	I've shown every interest. Every interest. I don't know what to say. Please can I come.

ETHEL	I really don't think
GRACIE	Please. Please. Just let me come.
ETHEL	It's going to be really boring.
GRACIE	Please don't go.
ETHEL	I've got to go. I want to go. It's important / I'll be back so soon. I'm so late already. Please. Can we have this conversation when I get back.
GRACIE	It's just a baby shower.
ETHEL	It's not just a baby shower. Not to me.
GRACIE	Please. Please just stay.
ETHEL	I'm going.
	ETHEL *goes to leave*.
	GRACIE *throws the rattle hard against the door.*
	ETHEL *spins around alarmed*.
GRACIE	I want a baby.
ETHEL	–
	What?
GRACIE	I want a baby. I think we should have a baby.
ETHEL	–
	Okay.
GRACIE	Okay?
ETHEL	Okay.
GRACIE	You want to?
ETHEL	Yep.
GRACIE	Okay then. Let's do it.
ETHEL	Okay.
	They kiss.
	GRACIE *becomes* JANIE.

25. PARTY

SARAH	I love a baby shower.
GRETA	Decorations are really quite something.
LINDA	Have you seen the nursery. It's yellow.
RITA	Did you bring a gift?
MICHAEL	No.
SUZIE	It's a nappy cake.
JOSEPH	Congratulations.
HANNAH	I'm not, it's not, it's not my baby shower.
HARRY	Good spread.
HANNAH	I'm just a bit fat.
VERITY	I must have seen that chin five times today.
CHARLOTTE	Six.
JACK	Someone at the door that might make seven.
SUZIE	It's a nappy cake.
JOHN	I went to pick up my bag, and, it's not mine. We've got the same bag!
CHARLOTTE	How do you feel about Marmite.
JACK	Indifferent.
CHARLOTTE	Indifferent! Me too.
JACK	Pure madness.
LUKE	Hang on I've got a camera somewhere.
LIZZIE	So we get to the M25 and he takes me clockwise! Clockwise. From Junction Twelve!
MILLY	Oh. Sorry, my gag reflex is absolutely terrible, that sausage roll /
KATE	Mine too!
LIBERTY	Heads-up, don't head to the nursery then, it is Ab-solutely vile.

PAUL	Don't suppose she's found out the sex yet.
GERTIE	No thank you I don't /
SAM	Eat gluten? Me neither.
RACHEL	Peter? Peter Leicester? It's Jen, Harriet's cousin. Harriet Lane. You dated her in what 1970.
PETER	Did I? So that's. No actually that's absolutely fine isn't it.
CELIA	Anyone for Champagne.
KIERAN	It's actually only Prosecco I'm afraid.
SUSAN	Whoopsie daisy there goes the hummus.
ERIC	Oh darling it's all over your shoes.
CAROLINE	Hello.
EMMA	Pleased to meet you, who are you?
CAROLINE	This is my house.
JACK	The mother, the mother the mother the mother is here.
LIZZIE	Can I, can I can I be the first to [touch your stomach].
CAROLINE	Oh. Um.
LINDA	Now darling, I didn't buy a present. I didn't know what would be right, BUT this here is the number of my hypnotherapist. She is an absolute wonder. Stopped my husband smoking. Cured my back pain. I've been to acupuncturists, Chinesey, what doyoumcallits, orthodontist, no what's the one I mean, what's the one I mean? Anyway SHE does births. Owe her both my granddaughters. No epidural. And none of us wants to be born into trauma, do we. Mother all drugged up on /
CAROLINE	Kieran.

SAM	Sausage roll, Caroline.
SARAH	Lovely nursery. Not every room can pull off yellow.
SEAN	Oop. No Prosecco for you. Fetal Alcohol syndrome /
LINDA	Is the father here?
CAROLINE	Sorry. I uh. Sorry. I'm so sorry.

–

–

–

Sorry everyone, I'm afraid everyone has to leave now. Absolutely. Terrible, misfortunate. Um... Thing is. What the thing is is. Is um... I suppose it's the nature of surprise parties really isn't it. I've actually got a plumber, coming, who, is, my husband, and is. Taking me away. To France. See.

SAM   Can't fly.

CAROLINE   On the Eurostar. Uh, because, that's actually. My birth plan. He's French, and he's very passionate about. And it helps with the passport. It's been *so* lovely to meet you all. So nice. So really really great. Um. But you really do all have to leave quite. Now.

They awkwardly shuffle out.

PAUL   Just gonna. Take. One for the road.

CAROLINE *is sat on the floor exhausted.*

KIERAN   Well I thought that was very rude.

CAROLINE   I did mean you too Kieran.

KIERAN   People made a tremendous effort and you
             were incredibly ungrateful.

CAROLINE   Ungrateful? Ungrateful for what? For the
             you-breaking-into-my-house? Or for
             whatever this is.

KIERAN   It's a nappy cake.

CAROLINE   I am so tired, Kieran. I'm so tired. I am eight
             months pregnant and I just worked a nine-
             hour shift. Do you even begin to understand
             that? Those. People.

KIERAN   Your family.

CAROLINE   I don't even like yellow, Bret painted it. And
             now it's the only thing my baby has left to
             remember its father by.

KIERAN   Bret's not, strictly, its father though. Is he.

CAROLINE   What?

KIERAN   Ah, sis, I don't care about any of that. I'm
             here for you whatever mistakes you make.
             That's what family is for isn't it?

CAROLINE   I'm not your sister, Kieran.

KIERAN   Yes you are. You are. Of course you.

CAROLINE   Do you have any idea what you've done? Do
             you have any idea what you've already cost
             me. Cost my baby? If a little dweeb in a
             shoulder bag had turned up ten years ago
             claiming to be my brother I'd have probably
             taken him in.

KIERAN   There's nothing more important than family.

CAROLINE   We are an island.

KIERAN   Me-and-you we?

CAROLINE   Get out of my house. Get out.

*Goes back to the floor and sits staring into
space. Stomach twinges. Settles. It's fine. No.
It's not fine. Goes for phone. Has to sit.*

(*Under.*) Fucksake.

KIERAN! Kieran. Kieran!

CAROLINE *breathes. She becomes* JAMES.

26. JAMES & BRET

JAMES   Talk more about that.

BRET   I think I've always felt like a bit of an
             outsider.

JAMES   Because of your hand.

BRET   No.

JAMES   Sorry.

BRET   I don't actually mind having something extra.
             It's feeling like I have less, feeling like I'm
             missing something that bothers. Bothers me.

             JAMES *and* BRET *become more intimate as*
             they become ETHEL *and* GRACIE.

27. ETHEL & GRACIE

Sunday morning laze.

ETHEL	Artificial insemination, or intrauterine insemination is a straightforward procedure where a fine tube or syringe containing the donor sperm is put inside the uterus during the woman's fertile time of the month.
	What? What are you smiling at?
GRACIE	I love seeing you in full teacher mode.
ETHEL	You can use sperm from an anonymous donor by going to a licensed fertility clinic.
	Or you can use a donor you already know.
GRACIE	Hey! We could get one of your new brothers to give us his spermies.
ETHEL	Ew. Gross!
	If you use sperm from a clinic, you won't know the identity of the donor. But, as of 2005, at eighteen the kid can find name, date of birth and last-known address. They can also join the Donor Sibling Link, which helps donor siblings exchange contact details if they would like to.
GRACIE	Which if they're anything like their mother, they certainly would.
ETHEL	I'm sort of assuming you want to carry it? Is that…?
GRACIE	I dunno.
ETHEL	Give your father the grandson he's always dreamt of.
GRACIE	Yeah.
ETHEL	Gracie you okay?
GRACIE	Yeah no I'm fine. Course I am.

ETHEL	I'm sorry I didn't mean to
GRACIE	No no no, just. I can't carry it can I. I'm probably a carrier for Huntington's.
ETHEL	Oh. No. I'm sure it's fine.
GRACIE	Huntington's is not fine.
ETHEL	You can find out. Do DNA test, that shows up congenital diseases. I've none, if you were wondering.
GRACIE	Ah well good for you. If only I had a long-lost trainspotter to sort it out for me.
ETHEL	I can ask Kieran if you like? We could sneak you in as a potential Barton Brooder.
GRACIE	Really?
ETHEL	Course. You'll have to pretend to think you're donor-conceived.
GRACIE	What I have to pretend to think I could be your sister.
ETHEL	Yeah why's that turn you on?
GRACIE	Mayb– / You know what actually no not at all.
	You'll sort it out for me?
ETHEL	Of course. So long as you admit my 'sibs' come in handy.

28. HENRY & TOM

HENRY	No sorry. I. I don't understand.
TOM	Okay. These here. Are chocolate buttons. You are gonna take your niece and nephew. Out to the chickens. And feed the chocolate buttons. To the chickens.
HENRY	Right. Yeah. Un.
TOM	And then we come back tomorrow. And...
HENRY	Yeah. And then they lay chocolate eggs.
TOM	Yeah.
HENRY	Right. That IS incredible. That is absolutely. Why don't you just feed them chocolate buttons all the time?
TOM	Why don't I feed them chocolate buttons all the time?
HENRY	Yeah.
TOM	Why don't I feed them chocolate buttons all the time?
HENRY	Yeah.
TOM	Sorry, I don't understand the question.
HENRY	?
TOM	You absolute cushion.

29. KIERAN & CAROLINE

CAROLINE *is in bed with her baby in the hospital.* KIERAN *arrives at the nurses' station and is talking to an unseen nurse.* CAROLINE *listens. Smiling.*

KIERAN   Hello I'm looking for Caroline Miller. Yeah she's my um… she's my. She's not actually.

CAROLINE   Hey

KIERAN   Hey, I'm probably the last person you want to see right now but. I just wanted to

CAROLINE   Sit

KIERAN   Ah. Ah. Yep.

CAROLINE   Thank you, for helping, that must have been, you didn't need to.

KIERAN   It wasn't, how I imagined seeing my first vagina, but, life's not always how you picture it, is it.

CAROLINE   Are you okay? It looked like you hit your head pretty hard when you passed out.

KIERAN   It does hurt a lot yes.

CAROLINE   Right.

KIERAN   I'm very sorry, Caroline. It's all been a bit of a project this family thing.

                I'm so sorry.

                I really am.

                We are twins but that really doesn't have to mean anything.

CAROLINE   I think we can work on what we are, but in the meantime, I think Iseult could do with an uncle.

KIERAN   You called her Iseult.

CAROLINE   No. It was a joke.

KIERAN   Ah.

CAROLINE   Mary. She's Mary.

                Mary Miller.

KIERAN   You called her Miller. Really.

CAROLINE   Yeah,

KIERAN   Samuel's name.

CAROLINE   My name. My name to give to anyone I please.

                Beat.

KIERAN   She healthy? Ten Fingers Ten Toes?

CAROLINE   Well actually.

                CAROLINE *digs out Mary's hands and
                shows* KIERAN. *He counts a few times*.

KIERAN   (Six) ...Oh so.

CAROLINE   Yep.

KIERAN   I thought you were artificially inseminated.

CAROLINE   Sixty-two-per-cent fail-rate so

KIERAN   Sixty-two per cent.

                Are you going to tell him?

CAROLINE   I will. Let's let it just be us family for a bit
                though

KIERAN   Family.

30. ETHEL & GRACIE

GRACIE   Is it normal? To come into hospital to get your DNA results? Didn't you get yours in a letter?

ETHEL   Yeah, it is weird, the guy was a bit um, weird, on the phone, I don't know. Look I'm sure it's nothing to worry about. Look. You could use one of my eggs and then maybe it would be sort of like it was both of ours?

I know this is the hospital your dad's in?

I do wish you'd let me see him.

He is here isn't he?

Shall we go together after the results?

I really hate to think of you always going on your own. You come back so sad. Eh? Please?

GRACIE   He's dead.

ETHEL   What?

GRACIE   He died.

ETHEL   When

GRACIE   A few months ago.

ETHEL   A few months ago?

GRACIE   Yep.

ETHEL   And you didn't tell me?

GRACIE   No

ETHEL   Why didn't you tell me?

GRACIE   (*Shrugs.*) You cross?

ETHEL   I'm a lot of things. I'm taken aback. Mainly I'm concerned.

Where've you been going all the times you've been going to see him?

GRACIE   To the house.

I just sit there. Look at things. It's so big. It's so big and full and empty. And I just sit there.

I felt like if I sat there long enough and willed it hard enough I'd think of something to say at the funeral. But I haven't yet.

It's funny you think those things just happen, funerals, they just sort of appear after someone dies. But if you don't organise them. They don't happen.

I got him cremated. No ceremony. Put him on the mantelpiece. In his castle. And we just sit there. Together. In the dark. I didn't pay the electric. I say more to him now than I think I ever did then. I told him about you. I told him a lot about you. I told him how you make me happy.

I tell him that you're beautiful, and kind and that you put baked beans in shepherd's pie which is really fucking weird but I pretend that I love it. And that when you're on the phone to British Gas you always spell your name in the phonetic alphabet like you think you're in the police or something. Echo Tango Hotel Echo Lima. I tell him that you think I've never told him about you because I'm embarrassed by you but I'm not embarrassed by you, I'm embarrassed by him. I tell him that you're the best thing, that you're the best thing that's ever happened to me in my whole life and I'm frightened by how much love you.

I'm frightened that if anyone or anything ever took you away from me I think that I'd kill them. I imagine killing them. I imagine tearing them apart. Sinking my fingers into their eye sockets and ripping off their checks.

Dislocating their jaw and pushing my hand
deep into the warmth of their gaping throat,
pushing arm-deep, puncturing their lungs
and snapping their rips from the inside until
I could squeeze all the blood out their heart
because that'd only be the same as what
they'd done to me.

I'm sorry that I didn't tell you.

ETHEL   I'm sorry that you didn't tell me.

GRACIE   I never should have kept it from you.

ETHEL   I'm drawing a line. I'm drawing a line and
from now on we're going to have to be
completely honest about everything with each
other. I think.

There's something I need to tell you too.

GRACIE   I don't want to have a baby.

ETHEL   Gracie I don't want to have a baby at all.

GRACIE   I hate babies.

ETHEL   Yeah. I don't hate babies. But I'd really hate to
have a baby. I'd really hate to have a baby in
my house all the time for like eighteen years.

GRACIE   That would be rubbish.

ETHEL   You're my. You're all the family I need.

GRACIE *is called.*

Your results. I can come in with you if you'd
like.

GRACIE   Really?

ETHEL   If you'd like.

GRACIE   No. That's okay. I... um. Don't need 'em do I.
If we're not. Having a baby.

ETHEL   Don't you wanna.

GRACIE   Nah. Just ruin everything. Wouldn't it.

31. BRET & BABY

BRET *is feeding the baby with difficulty but he's doing well.*

BRET   Oh wow.

Well you're very beautiful. You look like me.

I'm going to tell you a secret little one and I'm only going to tell you once. Through a very odd twist of fate. I'm not only your papa, I'm also your uncle. And I tell you something else, I'm gonna lie to you on that your whole life. I'm going to dedicate my whole life to making sure you never find that out. My beautiful baby girl. You're going to have the happiest life.

This little piggy went to market. This little piggy stayed at home. This little piggy had roast beef. This little piggy had none. This little piggy, was a bit of a whiny one to be honest with you. But this little piggy. Is gonna help you conquer the world.

The baby is uncomfortable.

Oh um… That better? You were a bit stifled there weren't you.

Who's your daddy?

The baby throws up over BRET.

You Millers.

Other Titles in this Series

Mike Bartlett
ALBION
BULL
GAME
AN INTERVENTION
KING CHARLES III
SNOWFLAKE
WILD

Jez Butterworth
THE FERRYMAN
JERUSALEM
JEZ BUTTERWORTH PLAYS: ONE
MOJO
THE NIGHT HERON
PARLOUR SONG
THE RIVER
THE WINTERLING

Caryl Churchill
BLUE HEART
CHURCHILL PLAYS: THREE
CHURCHILL PLAYS: FOUR
CHURCHILL PLAYS: FIVE
CHURCHILL: SHORTS
CLOUD NINE
DING DONG THE WICKED
A DREAM PLAY *after* Strindberg
DRUNK ENOUGH TO SAY
      I LOVE YOU?
ESCAPED ALONE
FAR AWAY
HERE WE GO
HOTEL
ICECREAM
LIGHT SHINING IN
      BUCKINGHAMSHIRE
LOVE AND INFORMATION
MAD FOREST
A NUMBER
PIGS AND DOGS
SEVEN JEWISH CHILDREN
THE SKRIKER
THIS IS A CHAIR
THYESTES *after* Seneca
TRAPS

Maud Dromgoole
3 BILLION SECONDS

Jodi Gray
PEEP
THROWN

debbie tucker green
BORN BAD
DIRTY BUTTERFLY
EAR FOR EYE
HANG
NUT
A PROFOUNDLY AFFECTIONATE,
PASSIONATE DEVOTION TO
      SOMEONE (– *NOUN*)
RANDOM
STONING MARY
TRADE & GENERATIONS
TRUTH AND RECONCILIATION

Rose Heiney
ELEPHANTS
ORIGINAL DEATH RABBIT

Tatty Hennessy
A HUNDRED WORDS FOR SNOW

Sam Holcroft
COCKROACH
DANCING BEARS
EDGAR & ANNABEL
PINK
RULES FOR LIVING
THE WARDROBE
WHILE YOU LIE

Vicky Jones
THE ONE
TOUCH

Anna Jordan
CHICKEN SHOP
FREAK
POP MUSIC
THE UNRETURNING
YEN

Lucy Kirkwood
BEAUTY AND THE BEAST
      with Katie Mitchell
BLOODY WIMMIN
THE CHILDREN
CHIMERICA
HEDDA *after* Ibsen
IT FELT EMPTY WHEN THE
      HEART WENT AT FIRST BUT
      IT IS ALRIGHT NOW
LUCY KIRKWOOD PLAYS: ONE
NSFW
TINDERBOX

Rose Lewenstein
COUGAR
DARKNET
FUCKING FEMINISTS
NOW THIS IS NOT THE END

Clare McIntyre
LOW LEVEL PANIC
MY HEART'S A SUITCASE
      & LOW LEVEL PANIC
THE MATHS TUTOR
THE THICKNESS OF SKIN

Sam Potter
HANNA

Jack Thorne
2ND MAY 1997
BUNNY
BURYING YOUR BROTHER IN
      THE PAVEMENT
A CHRISTMAS CAROL *after* Dickens
HOPE
JACK THORNE PLAYS: ONE
JUNKYARD
LET THE RIGHT ONE IN
      after John Ajvide Lindqvist
MYDIDAE
THE SOLID LIFE OF SUGAR WATER
STACY & FANNY AND FAGGOT
WHEN YOU CURE ME
WOYZECK *after* Büchner

Phoebe Waller-Bridge
FLEABAG

A Nick Hern Book

Mary's Babies first published in Great Britain as a paperback original in 2019 by Nick Hern Books Limited, The Glasshouse, 49a Goldhawk Road, London W12 8QP, in association with Jermyn Street Theatre, London and Oak Productions

Mary's Babies copyright © 2019 Maud Dromgoole

Maud Dromgoole has asserted her right to be identified as the author of this work

Designed and typeset by Nick Hern Books, London
Printed in Great Britain by Mimeo Ltd, Huntingdon, Cambridgeshire PE29 6XX

A CIP catalogue record for this book is available from the British Library

ISBN 978 1 84842 822 5